Cun

by Iain Gray

Lang**Syne**

PUBLISHING

WRITING *to* REMEMBER

LangSyne

PUBLISHING

WRITING *to* REMEMBER

79 Main Street, Newtongrange,
Midlothian EH22 4NA
Tel: 0131 344 0414   Fax: 0845 075 6085
E-mail: info@lang-syne.co.uk
www.langsyneshop.co.uk

Design by Dorothy Meikle
Printed by Ricoh Print Scotland
© Lang Syne Publishers Ltd 2012

ISBN 978-1-85217-110-0

Cunningham

Cunningham

MOTTO:
Over fork over.

CREST:
The head of a unicorn.

TERRITORY:
Ayrshire, Dumfriesshire, Renfrewshire.

Chapter one:

The origins of the clan system

by Rennie McOwan

The original Scottish clans of the Highlands and the great families of the Lowlands and Borders were gatherings of families, relatives, allies and neighbours for mutual protection against rivals or invaders.

Scotland experienced invasion from the Vikings, the Romans and English armies from the south. The Norman invasion of what is now England also had an influence on land-holding in Scotland. Some of these invaders stayed on and in time became 'Scottish'.

The word clan derives from the Gaelic language term 'clann', meaning children, and it was first used many centuries ago as communities were formed around tribal lands in glens and mountain fastnesses.

The format of clans changed over the centuries, but at its best the chief and his family held the land on behalf of all, like trustees, and the ordinary clansmen and women believed they had a blood relationship with the founder of their clan.

There were two way duties and obligations. An inadequate chief could be deposed and replaced by someone of greater ability.

Clan people had an immense pride in race. Their relationship with the chief was like adult children to a father and they had a real dignity.

The concept of clanship is very old and a more feudal notion of authority gradually crept in.

Pictland, for instance, was divided into seven principalities ruled by feudal leaders who were the strongest and most charismatic leaders of their particular groups.

By the sixth century the 'British' kingdoms of Strathclyde, Lothian and Celtic Dalriada (Argyll) had emerged and Scotland, as one nation, began to take shape in the time of King Kenneth MacAlpin.

Some chiefs claimed descent from

ancient kings which may not have been accurate in every case.

By the twelfth and thirteenth centuries the clans and families were more strongly brought under the central control of Scottish monarchs.

Lands were awarded and administered more and more under royal favour, yet the power of the area clan chiefs was still very great.

The long wars to ensure Scotland's independence against the expansionist ideas of English monarchs extended the influence of some clans and reduced the lands of others.

Those who supported Scotland's greatest king, Robert the Bruce, were awarded the territories of the families who had opposed his claim to the Scottish throne.

In the Scottish Borders country – the notorious Debatable Lands – the great families built up a ferocious reputation for providing warlike men accustomed to raiding into England and occasionally fighting one another.

Chiefs had the power to dispense justice

and to confiscate lands and clan warfare produced a society where martial virtues – courage,
hardiness, tenacity – were greatly admired.

Gradually the relationship between the
clans and the Crown became strained as Scottish
monarchs became more orientated to life in the
Lowlands and, on occasion, towards England.

The Highland clans spoke a different language, Gaelic, whereas the language of Lowland
Scotland and the court was Scots and in more
modern times, English.

Highlanders dressed differently, had different customs, and their wild mountain land
sometimes seemed almost foreign to people liv-
ing in the Lowlands.

It must be emphasised that Gaelic culture
was very rich and story-telling, poetry, piping, the
clarsach (harp) and other music all flourished and
were greatly respected.

Highland culture was different from
other parts of Scotland but it was not inferior or
less sophisticated.

Central Government, whether in London

*"The spirit of the clan means much
to thousands of people"*

or Edinburgh, sometimes saw the Gaelic clans as a challenge to their authority and some sent expeditions into the Highlands and west to crush the power of the Lords of the Isles.

Nevertheless, when the eighteenth century Jacobite Risings came along the cause of the Stuarts was mainly supported by Highland clans.

The word Jacobite comes from the Latin for James – Jacobus. The Jacobites wanted to restore the exiled Stuarts to the throne of Britain.

The monarchies of Scotland and England became one in 1603 when King James VI of Scotland (1st of England) gained the English throne after Queen Elizabeth died.

The Union of Parliaments of Scotland and England, the Treaty of Union, took place in 1707.

Some Highland clans, of course, and Lowland families opposed the Jacobites and supported the incoming Hanoverians.

After the Jacobite cause finally went down at Culloden in 1746 a kind of ethnic cleansing took place. The power of the chiefs was curtailed. Tartan and the pipes were banned in law.

Many emigrated, some because they wanted to, some because they were evicted by force. In addition, many Highlanders left for the cities of the south to seek work.

Many of the clan lands became home to sheep and deer shooting estates.

But the warlike traditions of the clans and the great Lowland and Border families lived on, with their descendants fighting bravely for freedom in two world wars.

Remember the men from whence you came, says the Gaelic proverb, and to that could be added the role of many heroic women.

The spirit of the clan, of having roots, whether Highland or Lowland, means much to thousands of people.

*Clan warfare produced a society where
courage and tenacity were greatly admired*

Chapter two:

Repelling the invader

From a descent that can be traced back to those Anglo-Normans who settled in Scotland in the years following the Norman Conquest of England in 1066, the Cunninghams became main players over the succeeding centuries in the drama and romance that is Scotland's story.

Hugo de Moreville, a descendant of Norman invaders who had intermarried with the Anglo Saxon nobility of England following the battle of Hastings, settled on lands granted to him in northern Ayrshire, on Scotland's west coast.

His power and influence increased to the extent that he was appointed to the premier post of Constable of Scotland, and in 1162 he granted some of his lands to a loyal retainer and kinsman known as Wernebald.

It is likely that Wernebald served de Moreville as one of his fighting men, or warriors, and that the land known as Cunninghame, in Ayrshire, was granted to him as reward for valued military service.

Dropping his Anglo-Saxon name, Wernebald adopted the name of his lands, giving rise to the family of Cunninghame, or Cunningham.

The spelling 'Cunninghame' appears to have given way to the spelling without a final 'e' in the late 17th to early 18th century and, for the sake of clarity, this is the form adopted in this brief narrative history of the family.

Some sources claim that 'Cunningham' itself derives from 'Cunedda', king of an ancient Celtic tribe known as the Votadini, and that it means 'courage in battle.'

'Cunedda' eventually became 'Cyning', then 'Cunning', while 'ham' signifies a hamlet or small village.

'Cunning' has also been taken to mean a coney, or rabbit, and it is perhaps significant that the heraldic arms of the Cunningham Earls of Glencairn feature two coneys.

An understandably rather less popular

explanation of 'Cunedda' is that it derives from 'Cinneidigh', meaning grim-headed, or ugly.

Whatever the derivation of the name and its adoption by Wernebald, it became a name to be reckoned with throughout the course of Scotland's turbulent history.

In 1263, Viking invasion threatened as the King of Scots, Alexander III, laid claim to the Hebrides. Warned that Alexander was prepared to wrest the islands from Norwegian control by force if necessary, King Hakon of Norway embarked with a mighty fleet from Bergen in July of that year.

His fierce band of sea raiders plundered and ravaged Kintyre, Bute, and Islay, before appearing off the west coast mainland township of Largs.

A storm blew many of the vessels onto the shore beneath the overhanging Cunningham hills on the night of September 30, and it was on top of these hills that the Scots king hastily assembled a force of militia that included Harvey Cunningham of Kilmaurs, a local land-holder.

A party of militia emerged from their high eminence the following morning and engaged in a skirmish with a band of Norsemen attempting to salvage precious cargo from their stricken vessels.

The Scots drove them back to their ships and returned that evening to gleefully loot the cargo.

Stung by the insult, King Hakon ordered a further attempt to retrieve the cargo the following day, October 1, resulting in what has become

known as the Battle of Largs, but which in reality consisted of a series of disorganised skirmishes.

The Norsemen were driven back to their vessels, however, and King Hakon died a few weeks later in Kirkwall, Orkney.

The threat to Scotland's western seaboard in general and invasion of the mainland in particular had been averted, and Alexander III confirmed Harvey Cunningham in his possession of the lands of Kilmaurs a year later in recognition of his bravery.

The battle is commemorated annually at Largs with the ceremonial burning of a Viking longboat.

Further grants of lands and honours were bestowed over the following centuries on the Cunninghams.

King Robert the Bruce gave Hugh Cunningham the lands of Lamburgton, in Ayrshire, in 1319 as reward for his military service at the battle of Bannockburn five years earlier, while he later acquired further lands at Stevenston, where he built Kerelaw Castle.

Although in ruins, the castle today is a tourist attraction.

An important marriage was made in 1399 when Sir William Cunningham married a daughter of Sir Robert Danielston of that Ilk. This marriage to Sir Robert's heiress brought lands at Finlaystone, at Langbank, in Renfrewshire, lands near Kilmarnock and Strathblane, and the estate of Glencairn, in Dumfriesshire.

It was from these Glencairn lands that the future earls took their name. Finlaystone, although recognised as the ancestral home of the Cunninghams, is now actually home to the present day MacMillan clan chief.

More lands were steadily acquired in Ayrshire, giving rise to the important Cunningham family branches of Craigends, Lainshaw, Bridgehouse, Caprington, Robertland, Auchinharvie, Milncraig, and Corsehill.

Lands were also acquired in both Lanarkshire and Midlothian, but these passed out of Cunningham ownership in the early decades of the 18th century.

Chapter three:

The bonnie fighters

Alexander Cunningham, who was made Lord Kilmaurs in 1462, and created 1st Earl of Glencairn by James III in 1488, had only a few short weeks to enjoy his new title before being killed in June of the same year at the battle of Sauchieburn, south of Stirling, and approximately on the same site of the battle of Bannockburn.

The earl was among a group of Scottish nobles who remained loyal to James in his struggle against other nobles who rebelled against his unpopular rule.

The rebels even had the tacit support of the king's own son, the future James IV.

The Earl of Glencairn was slain during the battle, while a mysterious stranger murdered James after being thrown from his horse while fleeing the battlefield. The monarch, ironically, had carried the sword of Robert the Bruce into battle.

The succeeding history of the Cunninghams in effect becomes a history of the exploits of the succeeding earls of Glencairn, who became known as 'bonnie fighters' not only because of their military prowess, but their zeal in defending their deeply held beliefs.

William, the 4th Earl of Glencairn, was among the Scots nobles captured after the disastrous battle of Solway Moss in November of 1542 and imprisoned for a time in England.

The battle had resulted after Henry VIII of England declared war on Scotland in response to his nephew James V's dogged refusal to sever his religious allegiance to the Papacy and alliance with France in favour of a closer alliance with England.

James died at Falkland Palace only a few weeks after Solway Moss and a matter of days before the birth of his heir, the future Mary, Queen of Scots.

The earl was released from captivity by Henry as one of the "assured Scots", with the understanding that he would support and press for

Henry's proposal for the future marriage of the infant Mary, Queen of Scots, to his young son and heir Prince Edward.

In January of 1544, however, the Earl of Glencairn entered into a contract with the earls of Lennox, Cassilis, and Angus, to give support to what was known as the national party in Scotland, which was opposed to English interference in Scottish affairs.

A staunch supporter of the Protestant Reformation and implacable foe of Mary, Queen of Scots, Alexander Cunningham, 5th Earl of Glencairn, had been opposed to her return to Scotland from France in August of 1561.

Known to posterity as 'the good earl', despite the fact that he was responsible for the wanton destruction of the royal chapel at

Holyrood, he was a firm friend of the fiery father of the Scottish Reformation, John Knox, and supported his return to Scotland from exile in 1554.

Knox is understood to have preached under a yew tree at the Cunningham property of Finlaystone, and the tree stands there to this day.

The earl mustered and marched a force of 2,500 men to Perth, in 1559, after Knox had preached a sermon that proved to be the spark that lit the militant flame of the Reformation, while he also played a leading role in the defeat of the ill-starred Mary at the battle of Langside, near Glasgow, in May of 1568.

He had also been appointed a member of the commission of regency following Mary's forced abdication in 1567.

James Cunningham, 7th Earl of Glencairn, was deeply involved in the numerous squabbles and battles that raged around who should have the care of James VI during his minority.

Along with the earls of Gowrie and Mar, the earl was instrumental in the infamous Ruthven Raid of August 22, 1581, when the 15-year-old

James VI was snatched from the care of the Regent, Arran.

The 9th Earl of Glencairn, William Cunningham, appears to have lived through particularly challenging times.

A supporter of Charles I until the monarch met his grim end on the executioner's block on Tower Hill, the earl's title was forfeited to the Scottish parliament but later restored when he rallied to the cause of the Covenant, which recognised the primacy to God, rather than the notion of the divine right of the Stuart monarchs.

His nation's independence came first, however, and following the Cromwellian invasion of Scotland in 1650 he lent his support to the cause of the exiled Charles II, embarking from 1653 until 1654 in what became known as Glencairn's Expedition – an ill-fated attempt to oust the English garrisons in Scotland.

An able military commander, the earl proved unable, however, to handle some of the wild Highland clansman he managed to rally to his support.

During a banquet held at Dornoch, Glencairn became embroiled in a fierce dispute with Sir George Munro over the discipline of the Highland forces the earl had raised.

The convivial atmosphere of the banquet soon descended into that of a rather less than civilised brawl, with the earl and Sir George literally having to be pulled apart as they engaged in a duel to defend their respective honours.

The earl was later forced, in the face of superior odds, to surrender to the forces of the able Cromwellian commander, General Monk, at Dumbarton.

Taken to England as a prisoner he was later allowed to return to Scotland, but promptly thrown into prison on suspicion of plotting against Scottish interests.

His constantly changing fortunes took a turn for the better following the Restoration of Charles II in 1660, when the monarch appointed him a Privy Councillor and, later, High Chancellor of Scotland.

Chapter four:

Patron of the bard

In the bitter battles that marked the conflict in Scotland between Crown and Covenant, John Cunningham, the 13th earl (1670-1703) eventually put religious conviction before personal interest.

Sickened by the brutal persecution of the Covenanters that he witnessed in his own lands in Ayrshire and Dumfriesshire, in his role of Commissioner of the Crown, he swung his powerful weight behind their cause.

The Cunninghams had always taken a great interest in the complex affairs of the church

in Scotland, and no less so than William Cunningham, the 13th Earl of Glencairn (1734-1775), who inspired Burns to verse.

The earl had become involved in a bitter and heated debate surrounding the Laigh Kirk, in Kilmarnock, over two rival preaching factions known as the Old Lichts (Lights) and the New Lichts.

A riot was sparked off when the well-meaning earl introduced a 'New Licht' minister to the touchy congregation, and the events surrounding the affair form the basis of Burns' poem *The Ordination*.

The earl also caused something of a scandal in disapproving aristocratic circles when he married the daughter of a lowly carpenter and fiddler who lived in Glasgow.

The marriage was a happy one, however, and their son, James, who succeeded to the title as 14th Earl of Glencairn on the death of his father, became a close friend and patron of Burns, providing the bard with invaluable help and encouragement.

Following the publication of the Kilmarnock edition of the poet's works, the earl managed to persuade the members of Edinburgh's influential Caledonian Hunt to subscribe towards the publication of the Edinburgh Edition.

Burns was devastated when his friend died on January 30, 1791, to the extent that he was moved to pen the brief, but moving *Lament for the Earl of Glencairn*:

> *The bridegroom may forget the bride*
> *was made his wedded wife yestreen;*
> *The monarch may forget the crown*
> *that on his head an hour has been;*
> *The mother may forget the child*
> *That smiles sae sweetly on her knee,*
> *But I'll remember thee Glencairn*
> *And a' that thou has done for me.*

Other notable Cunninghams include Alexander Cunningham, a historical writer who was British ambassador to Venice from 1715 to 1720, and the talented poet and writer Alan Cunningham, who was born at Blackwood, Dumfriesshire, in 1784.

Following his death in 1828, his family received support from Sir Walter Scott, one of his greatest admirers.

While not fighting external enemies in the form of Vikings or English armies, the Cunninghams were infamously involved in a bloody feud that spanned three centuries with their Ayrshire neighbours the Montgomerys, who held the title of Earls of Eglinton.

Some have even compared the rivalry that

existed to that of the Montagues and Capulet's of the Shakespearean drama *Romeo and Juliet* – without, of course, the love interest.

The trouble had started in 1448 when Sir Alexander Montgomery, a brother-in-law of Sir Robert Cunningham, was appointed to the post of Bailie of Cunningham – a title that the Cunninghams believed rightly belonged to Sir Robert.

Ten years later, in 1458, the position of bailie was restored to the Cunninghams under James II, as reward for their support in his struggle against the Douglas family.

This only served to intensify the feud, with the Montgomerys burning Kerelaw Castle in 1488 and the Cunninghams burning the Montgomery stronghold of Eglinton Castle, at Irvine, in 1528.

The feud reached a climax under the 7th Earl of Glencairn (1581-1629), when the Montgomerys blamed him for complicity in the murder of Hugh, the 4th Earl of Eglinton.

The Earl of Glencairn hotly denied any

involvement in the bloody affair and raised a legal action to counter the allegations against him.

While the action made its weary progress through the Scottish Parliament, scores of Montgomeries and Cunninghams were slain in a Mafia-style series of tit-for-tat killings.

The earl was eventually cleared of any complicity in the murder and the two families entered into talks in a vain attempt to reach an amicable accord.

But it was not until the marriage in 1661 of the Earl of Glencairn to Margaret Montgomery, a daughter of the 6th Earl of Eglinton, that the bitter feud finally came to an exhausted end.

The title of Earl of Glencairn has remained vacant for more than 200 years, following the death of the 15th earl in 1796, while numbers of Cunninghams in present-day Northern Ireland claim a descent from those Cunninghams who settled there when Sir James Cunningham was granted 500 acres of land in County Donegal during the Plantation of Ulster, from 1609 to 1613.

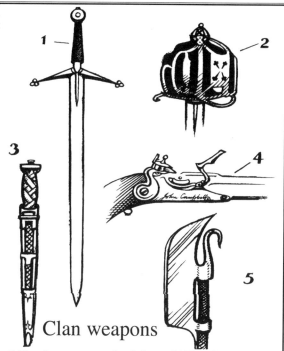

Clan weapons

1) The claymore or two-handed sword *(fifteenth or early sixteenth century)*
2) Basket hilt of broadsword made in Stirling, 1716
3) Highland dirk *(eighteenth century)*
4) Steel pistol *(detail)* made in Doune
5) Head of Lochaber Axe as carried in the '45 and earlier